SIGNIMALZ®

Created by Marni Kay Martinez
Illustrated by David R. Martinez

SIGNIMALZ®
Colors and Days of the Week

signimalz@outlook.com
www.signimalz.com
facebook.com/signimalz

COLORS

To sign <u>color</u>, place your fingers on your chin and wiggle them in place.

color

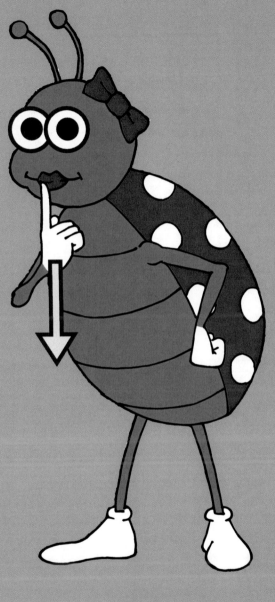

To sign <u>red</u>, place your index finger on your upper lip and slide down.

red

To sign <u>orange,</u> you "squeeze" your hand under your chin twice.

orange

To sign <u>yellow</u>, make the sign for "y" and wiggle it.

yellow

To sign <u>green</u>, make the sign for "g" and wiggle it.

green

To sign <u>blue</u>, make the sign for "b" and wiggle it.

blue

To sign <u>purple,</u> make the sign for "p" and wiggle it.

purple

To sign <u>pink</u>, make the sign for "p" and move it down from your lips.

pink

To sign <u>brown,</u> make the sign for "b" and slide your hand down the side of your cheek.

brown

To sign <u>black</u>, slide your straight index finger across your forehead.

To sign __white__, place your hand on your shirt with fingers extended. Move your hand away from your chest while pulling fingers together so that you have all your fingertips touching.

white

To sign <u>gray</u>, move your fingers back and forth through each other with your palms facing your chest.

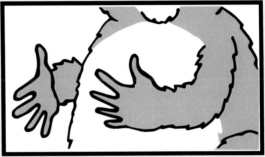

gray

Days of the Week

Start with your bent right elbow resting on the back of your left hand (which is held flat across your body – palm facing down). Bring your right index finger from pointing up in front of your shoulder, palm to the left, downward toward your left elbow. (Looks like the sun is setting.)

day

Start with two hands palms facing out in front of your shoulders. Move both hands down at the same time, sign ending by your waist.

Sunday

Another way to sign Sunday is have two hands facing out in front of your shoulders. Move both hands in an outward circle at the same time.

Sunday
(alternative version)

Make the sign for "m" and move it in a circle. (Your hand can face out or in.)

Monday

Make the sign for "t" and move it in a circle. (Your hand can face out or in.)

Tuesday

Make the sign for "w" and move it in a circle. (Your hand can face out or in.)

Wednesday

Make the sign for "h" and move it in a circle.

Thursday

Make the sign for “f” and move it in a circle. (Your hand can face out or in.)

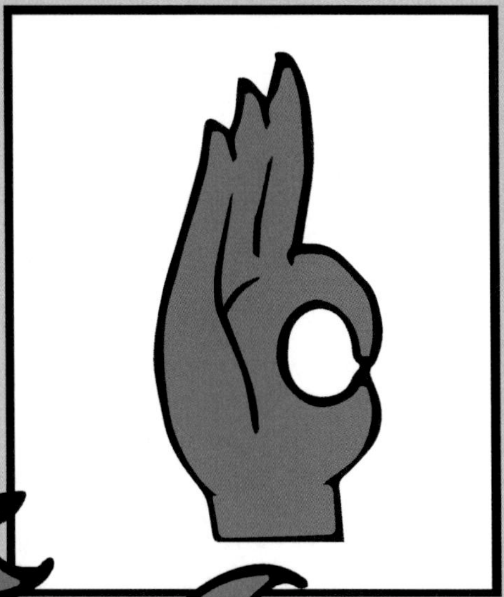

Friday

Make the sign for "s" and move it in a circle. (Your hand can face out or in.)

Saturday

Make the sign for "1". Slide it across your left hand, which is held palm facing up. (Looks like you are sliding your hand across one week on a calendar.)

week

Make the sign for "y" with both hands, palms facing up, bring them both down with a short movement in front of your body two times.

today

With a closed fist, put your thumb on your cheek. Move wrist forward, so that your thumb points out in front of your face.

tomorrow

With a closed fist, touch your thumb to the corner of your mouth. Move hand backwards, so that your thumb ends touching your face near your ear.

yesterday

About the Authors

Marni Kay Martinez was introduced to American Sign Language at an early age. Her mother, Sharon, worked with Deaf and Hard of Hearing students in an elementary school. As an elementary school student herself, Marni would go to school with her mom and communicate with the students often. Each time, she learned more signs and had so much fun "talking" with the students. As the years passed, Marni took American Sign Language (ASL) in High School and continued to learn ASL at the University of Central Florida (UCF). She graduated from UCF with a degree in Elementary Education. She then went on to pass her knowledge of sign language to students in her classes for over 15 years. The students and teachers at the school where she worked are the inspiration for this book.

David R. Martinez loves to draw. He is a licensed professional geologist and freelance illustrator who is inspired to create images that encourage creativity and produce smiles for kids of all ages.

Dave and Marni are a husband-and-wife team who enjoy spending time with their two children and look forward to collaborating on many projects together.

Made in the USA
Middletown, DE
17 November 2022